Orange Po

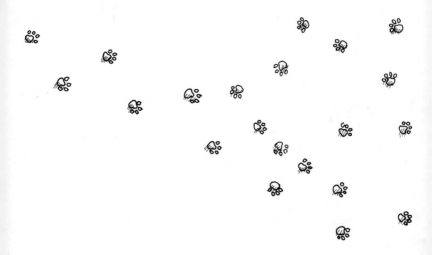

Orange
Paw Marks

Michelle Magorian

Illustrated by Jean Baylis

VIKING

FOR TOM

VIKING
Published by the Penguin Group
Penguin Books Ltd, 27 Wrights Lane, London W8 5TZ, England
Viking Penguin, a division of Penguin Books USA Inc.
375 Hudson Street, New York, New York 10014, USA
Penguin Books Australia Ltd, Ringwood, Victoria, Australia
Penguin Books Canada Ltd, 2801 John Street, Markham, Ontario, Canada L3R 1B4
Penguin Books (NZ) Ltd, 182–190 Wairau Road, Auckland 10, New Zealand

Penguin Books Ltd, Registered Offices: Harmondsworth, Middlesex, England

First published 1991
10 9 8 7 6 5 4 3 2 1

Text copyright © Michelle Magorian, 1991
Illustrations copyright © Jean Baylis, 1991

The moral right of the author has been asserted

Typeset in 12 on 14pt Century Schoolbook
by Rowland Phototypesetting (London) Ltd, 30 Oval Rd, NW1 7DE
Printed in Great Britain by Butler and Tanner Ltd,
Frome and London

A CIP catalogue record for this book is
available from the British Library

ISBN 0–670–82897–1

Contents

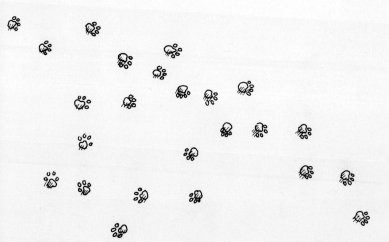

Woolly Fingers

My Auntie Lou knits cardigans –
She's not too good at it.
Her sleeves are always different lengths
And her buttons don't quite fit.

But they're always in bright colours
And what she knits I wear.
This one's the latest, it has stripes
And it makes the shoppers stare.

It's comfortable and keeps me warm,
It's thick and long and wide
And she's put pockets big enough
For loads of toys inside.

She's just knitted a hat for me
But it comes down to my chest,
So we use it on our birdcage
When our budgie needs a rest.

The Party

I don't want to go there,
I'll be sick on the floor,
I'll be sick like I was
When I went there before.

What if the jelly
Is too stiff to eat?
What if there's fat
On wobbly meat?

There might be bananas
All squishy and brown,
In custard to make sure
You swallow them down.

Please tell them I'm ill,
You just have to phone,
I'd much rather stay here
And play on my own.

Christmas Eve

I'm trying to sleep but my eyelids won't close
And I can't help but peep, for in front of my nose
Is a long woolly stocking that's red.
If I don't fall asleep Father Christmas won't come
And he won't eat the sandwiches made by my mum,
Or put toys at the end of my bed.

Upside Down

When I'm held upside down by my ankles,
The hallway's a different place.
I'm orbiting inside a rocket,
An astronaut floating in space.
Or I'm in a travelling circus,
A trapeze artist *extraordinaire*
Swinging above the terrified crowds
As I somersault high in the air.
Or maybe a monkey or chimpanzee
Who's escaped from the zoo into town,
The hallway's a very different place
When I'm held by my dad upside down.

What Sort of Song?

What sort of song would you like me to sing?
A rumpty-tumpty tune?
A song about summer or Christmas Day,
Or the stars, or sun, or moon?

I can sing you a song about a cat,
But you'd have to say mia-ow.
I can sing you a song about a dog,
But you'd have to shout bow-wow!

I can sing you a song to make you sleep,
Or one to keep you awake.
I can sing a song when candles are lit
On someone's birthday cake.

What sort of song would you like me to sing?
I can sing both high and low,
Songs I make up (they're very good),
And songs that you already know.

5

I'm Posting the Letters Today

I'm posting the letters today, I'm posting the
    letters today,
A letter that's blue to go on a plane,
A large white letter for my Auntie Jane,
A birthday card to be put on a train,
I'm posting the letters today.

I'm posting the letters today, I'm posting the
    letters today,
A letter from Mum to go over the sea,
A letter with drawings and kisses from me,
A letter Dad wrote while I sat on his knee,
I'm posting the letters today.

I'm posting the letters today, I'm posting the
   letters today,
Letters with stories of games I have played,
Letters describing the toys I have made,
Letters with blobs from my orangeade,
I'm posting the letters today.

Not Feeling Well

Mummy's too ill today
To take me outside to play.
So I'll stroke her head while she lies in bed
And smooth her headache away.

Hiccup!

Hiccup! Hiccup! Hiccup! I cannot stop saying
    Hiccup!
When I try to be quiet there's a hiccupy shout,
So I hold my breath till my cheeks swell out,
But as soon as I breathe more hiccups leap out,
Hiccup! Hiccup! Hiccup!

The Noisy Straw

I really can't help it if my straw makes a noise,
It's not me who's making it, it's it.
That gurgling and slurping, that hiccuping and
    burping
Is my straw enjoying every little bit!

Protecting Teddy

I'm holding my teddy this tight just in case
He's thrown in that washing machine.
Last time you put him there he had a fright
And he's not like *him* when he's clean.

He hates somersaulting around in that soap
And it always makes him shrink.
He'd come out some other colour, I know,
When I've just got used to him pink.

Mr Bean

Underneath the rhubarb leaves
Lives a frog called Mr Bean.
He likes it there because it's cool
And he knows he can't be seen.

I always creep and whisper
Like a tiny quiet mouse,
When I visit croaking Mr Bean
Inside his green-roofed house.

And if I crouch low on my heels
And push the leaves aside,
I can often watch him sit there
Till he hops away to hide.

Early Riser

Wake up! It's time to get up now,
The night and the moon have gone.
You can't want to sleep, there's daylight
    outside,
I've brought you some clothes to put on.

Open your eyes, don't be sleepy,
You don't want to stay here in bed.
You mustn't hide under the covers again,
It's morning, did you hear what I said?

It can't be too early, the birds are awake,
You don't really need all this rest.
I expect you're pretending you've gone back to
    sleep,
Are you sure you're not going to get dressed?

It's difficult trying to wake you,
Move over, I'll sit by your head.
And tell you the stories I know off by heart
Till you're ready to get out of bed.

Sad Music

Why does this music make me feel sad?
Why does it make me sit still?
Why does it make me lean on the wall
Under the window sill?

Don't turn it off, it's a sadness I like,
It's as though I don't have any friends.
I know it's not true, because I have you,
But I don't want to move till it ends.

Bus

Squashed up by the window
The sun burns my head.
It's winter outside
But Mum's cheeks have turned red.
More people crowd on
Shouting, ''Ere I was first!'
If any more squeeze in
The bus walls will burst.
We have to get off soon,
I wish we could fly
Over their heads
And out into the sky.
Instead we'll hold hands
And say lots of ''Scuse me's'
And I'll elbow my way
Through hundreds of knees.
And Mum will grip harder
And call out, 'Here goes!'
And I know someone heavy will
Stand on my toes.
And then she'll yell, 'Driver,
Hang on there, please!'
As we inch our way, sweating,
Towards the cool breeze.
And we'll stumble outside,
A fare and a half,
And stand on the pavement
And have a good laugh.
'I must learn to drive,'
My mum will say then,
But here comes our stop –
Will we make it again?

Cakes

A cake filled with jam,
A cake filled with cream,
A cake decorated
With an iced football team.

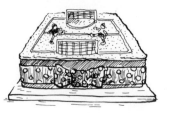

A cake with chocolate,
A cake light as air,
A cake like a railway train,
A cake cut square.

Small cakes with cherries,
Large cakes with flags,
Long cakes and tall cakes,
Stale cakes in bags.

Cakes in the window
For someone to eat,
Just the thing
For a tea-time treat.

Hard Work

Tying up laces is tiring –
Although I can make a good start –
I just get it right and then I pull tight,
But the bows that I tie fall apart.

Swopping

I'll swop you my car for your conker,
My conker I'll swop for your bike,
I'll swop you my bike for that book which I like,
I'll swop you my book for your honker.
My honker I'll swop for your star,
My star I'll swop for your bat,
I'll swop you my bat for your fireman's hat,
I'll swop you my hat for your car.

Hugs

I've three special hugs for you, Granny,
Hug one, hug two, and hug three.
This hug's from rabbit,
This hug's from hippo,
And this snuggly huggle's from me.

Sun Day

Asleep in the deck-chair in the afternoon sun,
Knees up, mouth open and sandals undone.
Shadows in the garden, and one buzzing bee
And Daddy digging worms up for the birds'
    Sunday tea.

Shy

Has he gone yet, that man with the laugh?
If not I'd rather stay here.
Keep standing still so I can hide behind your legs,
Don't let him come too near.

Don't move away because I've pressed my face
Hard into the back of your knees.
I've closed my eyes and I'm wishing him away,
Don't make me talk to him, please.

It's not that I'm scared and it's not that I'm rude.
Can't I say hello another day?
His voice is too loud and he's much too tall.
Tell him that we don't want him to stay.

Red!

Red socks, red shoes,
I like red!
Red scarf, red hat
On my head.
Red trousers, red shirt,
Red stripy sweater.
There is no other colour
I like better.

The Hat

When I wear this hat I'm strong and I'm brave,
I can rescue captured people, just like that.
I have dangerous adventures, I tell people what
    to do,
I'm the captain, I'm the boss, in this hat.

Balcony Picnic

Up on the balcony, high in the air,
Drinking fizzy orange in an old deck-chair,
The washing hangs above me, the traffic's far
    below,
And Mum is carrying sandwiches, but on tiptoe.

My little sister's sleeping so it's just Mum and me,
And we're having chocolate fingers for our
    picnic tea,
And sandwiches with jam, buns and sausage
    rolls,
And ice-cream and jelly in yellow plastic bowls.

We mustn't laugh too loud in case my sister
    wakes,
So we're whispering very quietly and eating
    fairy cakes.
Nobody can see us watching planes fly by,
Sitting here and eating our picnic in the sky.

What Would You Do?

What would you do if your sausages flew
And your peas danced around on the plate?

Would you still eat if your carrots had feet
And twirled one leg raised on a skate?

What would you drink if your tea turned pink
And started to sing a loud song?
Would you join in the chorus along with the tea?
Would you have a wild dance with the
    friendliest pea?

Or skate with the carrot or skip with the fruit,
Or land with a sausage by egg parachute?

I know what I'd do – with the loudest 'Yahoo!'
I'd turn cartwheels and yell out, 'How's that!'
Then I'd run out and play with my dinner all day
And what would I eat? Why, my hat!

Exercising with Grandma

Exercising with Grandma,
In our tights on the sitting-room floor.
Bending and stretching and lifting our feet,
Swaying and raising our arms to the beat,
And stretching a little bit more.

Exercising with Grandma,
Lying now on my side,
Toes to the ceiling, knee bent and straight,
Our tummies rumbling from something we ate,
And we sit with our legs out wide.

Exercising with Grandma,
Makes me sweat and I ache and I puff,
With her, 'Now to the right and the left and again,
And a seven and eight and a nine and a ten',
Till I'm tired and have had quite enough.

Exercising with Grandma
Is fun, but it's nice when we rest.
We lie back as warm as we are when there's sun,
And listen to music when stretching is done.
That is the bit I like best.

Birthday Surprise

A cake with raspberries and cream inside
And a marzipan pig on top,
That's what my daddy made me
To eat with lemonade pop.

That's what he made in secret
While I was asleep in bed,
With four coloured candles stuck round the pig
And a raspberry hat for his head.

Rushing

Rush, rush, rush, rush,
Do we have to go so fast?
In a hurry, in a hurry,
Does it matter if we're last?
Quick, quick, quick, quick,
My forehead and my ankles ache.
Speedy, speedy, speedy, speedy,
Can't we stop and have a break?
Run, run, run, run,
We can catch another bus.
Puff, puff, puff, puff,
No breath left at all in us.
Slow, slow, slow, slow,
Things to look at while we wait.
Chat, chat, chat, chat,
It's much nicer being late.

27

My Terrible Sister

My sister is two and she's too much of a baby,
She's always getting in my way.
She makes a lot of noise and breaks my
    favourite toys,
I wish she'd leave me on my own to play.

My sister is two and she's too much of a
    nuisance,
She kicks me hard and sometimes pulls my
    hair.
And when I shout, 'Clear Off!' I'm the one who
    gets told off –
She gets a hug and kiss, which isn't fair.

My sister is two and she's too too clumsy.
Don't you think it's time she went to bed?
I know it's still the morning, but I'm sure I saw
    her yawning,
I'll go and get a pillow for her head.

My sister is two but she thinks she is grown up,
She is always wearing boots which are too
    large.
She's trying to look older but her gumboots trip
    her over
And she shouts at me and stamps when I'm in
    charge.

My sister is two and she's too too messy,
She covers all my books with paint and glue.
Mum says it is her age, I'd like to put her in a
    cage,
My terrible sister who's two.

Wind

Outside my window, the wind blows hard,
Tearing at the leaves in the trees.
Bending branches far till they tap against the
    glass,
Swishing loud like stormy, tossing seas.

The sky is dark, the rain makes mud and pools
Trickling cool and silver on the pane,
Splattering the dirt track, and drumming on the
    roof,
And starting tiny rivers in the lane.

It's a wild wild night, I can hear the chimneys
    howl.
There's a whistling and a moaning in the air.
The quilt's up to my ears but I'm pretending I'm
    outside,
Running with the wind inside my hair.

Goodbye Room

Goodbye Room,
I wish and I wish I could stay,
But outside there's a van, and it's filled to the
    roof,
Because this is removal day.

Goodbye Room,
I don't want to leave you at all.
Goodbye window and goodbye cupboard
And goodbye marks on the wall.

Goodbye Room,
I'm going to live somewhere new.
They say my next room will be sunny and big,
But I'd much rather sleep here in you.

Kitchen Secret

Squashing the dough with my fingers,
Rolling it into a ball,
Tearing up bits and squeezing them tight,
Making them round and small.

Pressing them flat on the table,
Watching Dad flour the tray,
Pushing the pastry inside the cups
And wondering if it's too grey.

Spooning in plenty of apple,
Putting on pastry tops,
Pressing them round so they look like pies
As good as you buy in the shops.

Shutting Mum out of the kitchen,
Keeping it as a surprise,
Closing the door of the oven tight
And hoping the pastry will rise.

That Baby

That baby is always making you tired,
Perhaps we should send it away,
Then you can have a lovely long sleep
And we can go out and play.

Evening Strokes

Do you have to brush my hair so hard?
You're making my head sore.
Tomorrow, after I've slept on it,
It will only look the same as before.

The Goblin

It's not my fault my coat is on the floor
In the cupboard under the stairs.
It's far too dangerous for me to hang it up
Because of the goblin who glares.
He hides in the dark with his red bulbous eyes,
Ready to pounce on me.
I have to wait till I think he's asleep,
Hold my breath and count to three.
Then I open the door as quick as I can,
I haven't the time to be neat.
If I stay too long the goblin will leap
And stamp on me with his flat feet.
He could kidnap me and eat me alive,
But nobody really cares.
They still say I've got to hang up my coat
On the hook fixed under the stairs.

The Voyage

This box is a boat,
The carpet's the sea,
Those patterns are fishes,
That armchair's the quay.

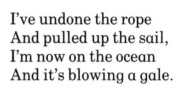

I've undone the rope
And pulled up the sail,
I'm now on the ocean
And it's blowing a gale.

The wind's loud and fierce,
The waves leap up high,
But I'm sailing her well
In the dark thundery sky.

The sun has appeared,
I've sailed through the storm.
The sky has turned blue
And the air has grown warm.

Look, there are some stars!
I'll stay here the night
And sleep on the waves
Beneath the moon's light.

37

Wet

It's wet, wet, wet,
And my mackintosh is dripping,
Wet, wet, wet,
And my wellingtons are slipping,
Wet, wet, wet,
And the wind is fiercely whipping
Through the trees.

Wet, wet, wet,
Heavy hail-stones are dropping,
Wet, wet, wet,
On our heads and all the shopping,
Wet, wet, wet,
Sending muddy puddles hopping,
Wet, wet, wet,
Up to my knees.

Too Many Choices

I'm swaying this way from foot to foot
To help me concentrate.
I don't know whether to play outside
Or draw circles round a plate.

There's paper and large fat crayons indoors,
But I'll rock till I decide
Whether to play in the sand-pit
Or colour in patterns, inside.

This thinking is making me more and more tired.
I wish I knew which I liked best.
If I don't know what to start doing next, soon,
I will have to lie down for a rest.

No Time

This button goes inside this hole, that button
  goes inside there,
I've put both my socks on and tucked in my vest,
I've pulled up my trousers, I'm nearly all
  dressed,
I have even combed back my hair.

This wellie goes on the left foot, this wellie goes
  on the right,
There's no time for me to eat breakfast today,
There's wind on the hill and it might go away
And I won't get to fly my new kite.

Fuss Pot

Chocolate biscuits in the sun
Have a tendency to run
And they melt around your fingers in a mess.
If there's one thing I can't stand,
It's having sticky hands,
Especially when I'm wearing my best dress.

I hope you'll beg my pardon
If I don't eat in your garden.
It's not that I'm ungrateful or unkind.
Birthday parties in the sun
Are supposed to be good fun,
But I'd rather stay indoors if you don't mind.

41

Hopping

I can hop on one leg,
I can jump on two,
I can hop on the other one,
Can you do it too?

I can hop over a rope
On the spot if I like,
I can hop with both legs fast
As if I'm riding a bike.

I can hop on a bended knee,
Hopping very low.
I can hop up very high,
Stretching every toe.

I can hop and hold one foot
And lah a hopping tune,
And I can hop in a hopping race
With an egg and spoon.

Turning

This is my turning in circles game.
I turn till the ground starts to tip.
Then when I fall over and everything spins,
I pretend I'm at sea on a ship.

Indoor Game

When I lean out of the window
And the rain is falling fast,
I catch the drips with my fingertips
And as the cars whizz past,
I can see the women running by,
As splashes leap in the air,
On their high heels avoiding the wheels,
Holding newspapers over their hair.

It's True!

Grandpa's coming to the beach with us!
And he's bringing me a bucket and spade.
He told me he'll dig me a car in the sand,
The biggest car he's ever ever made.

He says it's years since he played in the sand,
Years seems a long time to me.
Mummy's bought swimming trunks just like
    mine
For him to wear when we paddle in the sea.

It's true, it's true, it's really really true!
He told me so it isn't just a dream.
He's coming to the beach with me and Mummy,
And Daddy, and we're having ice-cream.

Tomato Sauce

Tomato sauce, tomato sauce,
On my sausages of course,
That's my favourite, *and* on toast,
That's what I like eating most.

Mobiles

The breeze blows in through the window,
Flings the mobiles from side to side,
Makes houses jump upwards and flowers spin
    round
And cats and roosters collide.

Sprinkled

Running away from the garden spray,
Dashing back as it spins,
Trying to beat it again as it whirls
And being the one who wins.

Dancing around on the cool wet ground,
Grass sticking up through my toes,
Being splashed hard when I'm not fast enough
From my feet to my knees to my nose.

Drips in my hair, but I don't care.
It's good getting wet in the sun.
Having a race with the sprinkler
And seeing how fast I can run.

Lazy Morning

Mummy is lazy one morning a week,
She spreads newspapers over the bed.
Daddy brings porridge and jam on a tray
And coffee and hot toasted bread.

We cuddle up close while she reads to herself,
And give her a hug and a squeeze.
That makes her smile, and she squeezes us back
And her newspapers slide off her knees.

Daddy then reads me a story I like.
It's good when he acts all the parts,
And though Mummy's reading, we know when she listens
For her newspaper shakes and her giggling starts.

Daddy's not busy and Mummy's not busy,
So until all the papers are read,
One morning a week we all stay together
Eating and reading in bed.

Winter Morning

It's much too cold
To get out of my warm bed,
So I'll watch my breath
Rise out of it instead.

Waiting

When is he coming?
Will he be long?
I still cannot see him,
I hope nothing's wrong.
Perhaps he's got lost.
Perhaps you should phone.
I've been watching for hours
Here on my own.
He might have forgotten
He's coming to stay.
Are you sure he'll remember
That today is the day?

Snow

Look, Old Teddy, see the snow
Falling on the window sill,
See it gliding to the ground,
Covering the road and hill.

Feel, Old Teddy, with your paw
The coldness of the window pane,
Watch me blow onto the glass
And draw a picture of a train.

See, Old Teddy, how the trees
Are bending under all the snow,
Even footsteps sound much softer,
Look how all the cars go slow.

Now, Old Teddy, here's your coat,
Your stripy mitts and bobble hat,
I'll wrap you up to keep you warm
And then we'll both be snug and fat.

Old Teddy, if you hold your face up
And let the cold flakes touch your nose,
You can feel them melt away,
That's what I like, when it snows.

Summer Ride

Riding on a roofless bus
With Julia,
Sitting in the front. Just us.
How cool we are.

Spring

Sunlight on the garden,
Flowers on the hill,
The bathroom window open
And my elbows on the sill.

Blossom in the trees,
Buds and birds and leaves,
Sun so warm against my face
I've rolled up both my sleeves.

Singing from the kitchen,
A pale blue sky,
Daffodils among the grass
And washing out to dry.

Don't Go!

Don't go!
Stay here!
I want you
To be near.
I'll scream!
I'll shout!
If you dare
Go out.
Why can't
You stay?
Go to work
Some other day.
You wait,
You'll be
Very sorry
You left me.
I'll stamp!
I'll cry!
If you leave
And say goodbye.

You've gone!
Gone away!
Oh all right,
I'll go and play.

Ssh!

It's a very quiet day,
I can hardly hear a sound
Except the baby breathing in his sleep.
There's no shout or sneeze or cough,
The radio's switched off,
Not a screeching car or siren, wail, or bleep.

It's a very quiet day,
It makes me want to whisper
And pad about in socks instead of shoes.
It makes me want to look
At pictures in a book,
Or close my eyes and lie down for a snooze.

Babies

Babies are funny.
They don't speak a lot.
They can't drink from cups
Or sit on a pot.

They like to grip fingers.
They like milk from Mummies.
They like having raspberries
Blown on their tummies.

They like being cuddled
And kissed on the head.
But they don't say a lot,
They just dribble instead.

Party Frock

My mother wore this when she was a girl,
I'm wearing it today because I like to hear it
   swirl,
These bits are mauve and these bits are pink.
I know it's rather long but it's good on me I
   think.
I'll lift up the skirt so you can see underneath.
This is called net and I've a petticoat beneath.
I'll turn so I can show you my taffeta bow
Taffeta is shiny (just in case you didn't know).
It wasn't like this when we found it in a box;
It was covered in dust with some other party
   frocks.

Then it was washed, that's why it looks so new,
The net's been stiffened and my mother ironed
   it too.
Watch how it lifts when I twirl it this way,
I'm glad it's my party, I can wear it all day.
I know I like jeans and sneakers and shirts
But I like silver shoes too and frocks with skirts.
You think I look funny but really don't you
   wish
You had a dress you could make go swish?

The Quarrel

I'm never going round to her place again,
And I won't have her coming here to play.
She hates all my games and I hate her.
I don't want to see her today.

She pulled my hair, I kicked her leg,
She pushed me and gave me this bite.
Those teeth marks are hers. Look at my arm!
It's her fault we had a big fight.

She'd better say sorry, she'd better.
I am not saying sorry to her.
I'll play by myself and if she comes near
I'll pretend I'm a tiger and go grrruh!

Monster

Grandad lets me stay up late.
Why don't you?
Grandad gives me sweets in bed.
You should too.

Grandad never tells me 'No'.
It's always 'Yes'.
I never have to brush my teeth
Or clear away my mess.

Grandad does what he is told
And he gives me money.
Grandad gives me what I ask for,
I'm his honey bunny.

Grandad never tells me off,
No matter what I do.
Even when I smash his plates
And stuff things down his loo.

Grandad lets me kick him hard,
He never says I'm bad.
I'd rather stay with him than you,
Silly Mum and Dad.

Orange Paw Marks

Orange paw marks from the paint tin,
Orange paw marks in the yard,
Orange paw marks in the kitchen
And past the fire-guard.

Orange paw marks on the table,
Orange paw marks on the floor,
Orange paw marks on the high
chair,
Orange paw marks to the door.

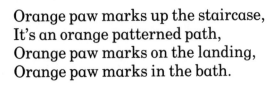

Orange paw marks up the staircase,
It's an orange patterned path,
Orange paw marks on the landing,
Orange paw marks in the bath.

Orange paw marks in our bedroom,
On the patchwork eiderdown,
Orange paw marks in the cot
And on my sister's dressing-gown.

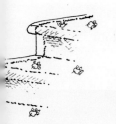

Orange paw marks on the carpets,
'Orange paw marks!' my Dad wails
As he follows all the winding,
Crossing orange paw mark trails.

When you leave the lid off paint
And you have a nosy cat,
The result is orange paw marks,
Oh, please remember that!

61

Please Don't Close My Bedroom Door

Please don't close my bedroom door.
Leave the hall light on.
Then I won't be scared of being
Alone when you have gone.

I shall see red elephant,
And Cecil, my white bear,
And Pinkest, my pink woolly pig,
Instead of shadows there.

But if you shut the door I'll hear
The monster's creaking feet,
And I will have to hide all night
Underneath the sheet.

Munch Munch

In my bath are three yellow ducks
And a hungry crocodile with teeth.
He chomps through the waves as the ducks
   swim away
And dives to the depths underneath
Where he lurks and he watches till he's ready to
   pounce,
Then he opens his mouth for a munch,
For there's nothing old Ferdinand my crocodile
   likes more
Than a tasty yellow duck for his lunch.

A Special Occasion

My shoes are brushed,
My hands are clean,
My hair is combed,
And I have 'been'.
I have not moved
From this hard seat,
Because you said
I must stay neat.
Can't I move soon?
When can I play?
Will it last long,
This wedding day?

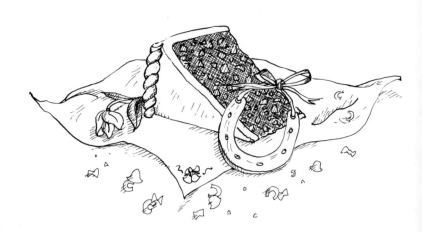

The Present

But you told me never to tell a lie,
So why do you want me to say
That I love this green jumper and thank you so
    much,
When I'd much rather throw it away?

I can't say it's nice, I can't say I'm pleased,
It's the horriblest jumper I've seen.
It has horrible sleeves, it's a horrible shape,
It's the horriblest bright sort of green.

It'll be a huge fib if I tell her
That I'm pleased that she made it for me.
And do I *have* to wear it outside
When we visit her place for tea?

Wiggling

I've tried to wiggle every tooth,
But I've only got stiff teeth.
Are you sure that there are grown up ones
Hidden underneath?

When I Grow Up

When I grow up
What shall I be?
Will I be different
Or still be me?

Newborn

His skin is very soft.
He looks so comfortable tucked up.
Am I really his big brother?
Will he think I am grown up?

Can I hold him in my arms?
I like to feel him near.
If I talk to him and tell him things
Do you think that he will hear?

He's closed his eyes again.
Is it still all right to touch?
Do you think he likes my kisses?
Why does he sleep so much?

Is being born hard work?
Is that why he's asleep?
His feet and hands are tiny.
Is he really ours to keep?

We'll make sure he stays warm
And I'll show him how to swim
And walk and play and give him hugs.
When I was born, was I like him?

Rain Music

The rain plays a tune
In the buckets
That are standing
On the landing,
Plays a tune.
The rain plays a tune
In the bowl
That is standing
On the landing,
Plays a tune.
The rain plays a tune
With the drips
From the ceiling
Which is peeling,
Plays a tune.
The rain plays a tune
With the drips
That go plip,
Plays a tune, plays a tune
With the drops
That go plop,
Plays a tune, plays a tune
With the drips and the drops
And the plip plip plops
And the drops and the drips
And the plop plop plips,
Plays a tune, plays a tune, plays a
plop.

Cross

I don't want to answer any more questions,
I've already answered them all.
If I'm asked them again, I'll get a red pen
And draw pictures all over the wall.

Index of First Lines

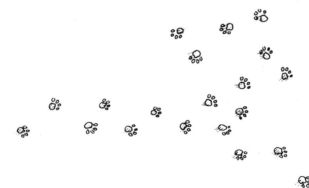